Following an era of offensive juggernauts, Major League Baseball has entered a new age of unhittable moundsmen. Whereas sluggers once dominated, young hurlers armed with 100-mph fastballs, knee-buckling curveballs and devastating sliders now rule the planet. People called 2010 the "Year of the Pitcher," and it's easy to see why, with low run totals, high strikeouts rates, and complete games and no-hitters galore. With more great young arms developing, the trend doesn't appear to be ending anytime soon. Yes, it's time to fear the pitcher.

But how exactly do you rank the most feared hurlers? Do you start with the guy who throws the hardest? Strikes out the most batters? The guy who can pinpoint his pitches as if hitting the bull's eye on a dartboard? Perhaps he just plain *looks* like the baddest guy around when he's on the hill. Debating the qualities of players has always been one of the most cherished aspects of baseball. Maybe you love Cliff Lee's mastery of the strike zone and ability to keep hitters off balance. Or perhaps you favor Tim Lincecum's explosive delivery and knack for making batters look foolish by swinging at nothing but air. Whomever you prefer, there's no question that even the best batters get butterflies standing in the box against baseball's top pitchers.

Hopefully you'll spend plenty of time creating your own list of feared pitchers and watching your favorite aces earn their way onto it. But what follows is our ranking. So turn the page and start comparing.

1. ROY HALLADAY

Team: Philadelphia Phillies
Throws: Right
Uniform #: 34

When Roy "Doc" Halladay hit the trade market in 2009, it was no wonder Philadelphia jumped at the chance to acquire the 6-foot-6, 230-pound right-hander. During the past decade, Halladay has been consistently excellent, stifling the opposition and pitching deeper into games than any other hurler in baseball. In fact, Halladay has led his league in complete games several times. "His game plan, his work ethic ... it's second to none," says Mets third baseman David Wright. "He has some of the best stuff in the game — as far as attitude and preparation, I think he *is* the best in the game — and that makes him elite." En route to his second Cy Young Award in 2010, the ace threw a perfect game against the Florida Marlins in the regular season and a no-hitter against the Cincinnati Reds in his first career playoff start — just the second no-hitter in playoff history.

THE MAJOR LEAGUE BASEBALL
25 MOST FEARED PITCHERS

Written by the editors of Major League Baseball

MAJOR LEAGUE BASEBALL PROPERTIES, INC.

CONTENTS

The Major League Baseball 25 Most Feared Pitchers was developed, written and designed by MLB PUBLISHING, the publishing department of Major League Baseball Properties, Inc.

Printed in the U.S.A.

First Printing: July 2011

ISBN-13: 978-0-9776476-5-1

ISBN-10: 0-9776476-5-x

PHOTO CREDITS: Kennedy/Philadelphia Phillies/MLB Photos (Halladay cover, p. 4); Shaw/Getty Images (Wilson cover, Hernandez p. 6, Kershaw p. 18, Bell p. 36); Ivins/Boston Red Sox/MLB Photos (Lester cover); Tringali/MLB Photos (Lee cover, Rivera cover, Lee p. 10, Rivera p. 12); Mangin/MLB Photos (Lincecum cover, Wilson p. 24, Cain p. 30, Feliz p. 32, Wilson back cover); Pilling/MLB Photos (Lincecum p. 7, Strasburg p. 34, Halladay p. 42); Ehrmann/Getty Images (Johnson p. 8); Grieshop/MLB Photos (Lester p. 11); Halip/Getty Images (Verlander p. 14, back cover); McIsaac/Getty Images (Sabathia p. 16, back cover); Spinelli/MLB Photos (Weaver p. 17, Haren p. 28); Terrill/Pool/MLB Photos (Price p. 20); Pensinger/Getty Images (Jimenez p. 22); Cox/Getty Images (Wainwright p. 23, Greinke p. 29); Ferrey/Getty Images (Soria p. 26); Vishwanat/Getty Images (Carpenter p. 35); Petersen/Getty Images (Chapman p. 38); Dunn/Getty Images (Broxton p. 39); How/Getty Images (Wood p. 40); Scharfman/Sports Imagery/Getty Images (Gibson p. 41); NBLA/MLB Photos (Larsen p. 41, Haddix p. 42, Vander Meer p. 43); MLB Photos (Morris p. 43)

"He expects to finish the game, and that's not very common. It's like he's disappointed if he doesn't throw all nine innings."

—David Wright

2. FELIX HERNANDEZ

Team: Seattle Mariners
Throws: Right
Uniform #: 34

Compared to other pitchers around the AL, Felix Hernandez is royalty. Dubbed "King Felix," Hernandez garnered 2010 American League Cy Young honors despite winning just 13 games. He earned the crown by posting a Major League–leading 2.27 ERA and striking out a whopping 232 batters while throwing a league-high 249.2 innings. The award may have cemented Hernandez's status as a household name before he even turned 25, but his achievement was far from unexpected. As a 14-year-old in Venezuela, he had captured the attention of scouts, making his debut with the Mariners just five years later, at age 19, in 2005. Since his teenage years, the ace has been a force in the Seattle rotation. Hernandez took the fast track to stardom, collecting his 1,000th career strikeout during the 2010 campaign. Every team in Major League Baseball would be thrilled to have the 6-foot-3, 225-pound right-hander with a mid-90s sinking fastball highlighting its roster.

FACTOID
Fourth-youngest pitcher ever to reach 1,000 strikeouts

At just 5 foot 11 and 165 pounds, Giants ace Tim Lincecum may seem an unlikely candidate to dominate the Big Leagues, but his resume stands as tall as any pitcher's in the game. Before his 28th birthday, "The Freak" — a nickname that fits his unique personality as much as his inimitable elastic pitching motion — had already collected two National League Cy Young Awards, three NL strikeout titles and a World Series ring. "Lincecum, obviously, is a dominating pitcher," Cardinals left fielder Matt Holliday says. "He'll probably consistently lead the league in strikeouts by a large margin. That's always an indicator of dominance." Through his first four seasons, Lincecum struck out 907 batters and carried his fearsome fastball into the 2010 postseason. In six playoff starts, he fanned 43 batters and outdueled lefty Cliff Lee — another one of baseball's most feared pitchers — not once, but twice during the Giants' run to the title.

Team: San Francisco Giants
Throws: Right
Uniform #: 55

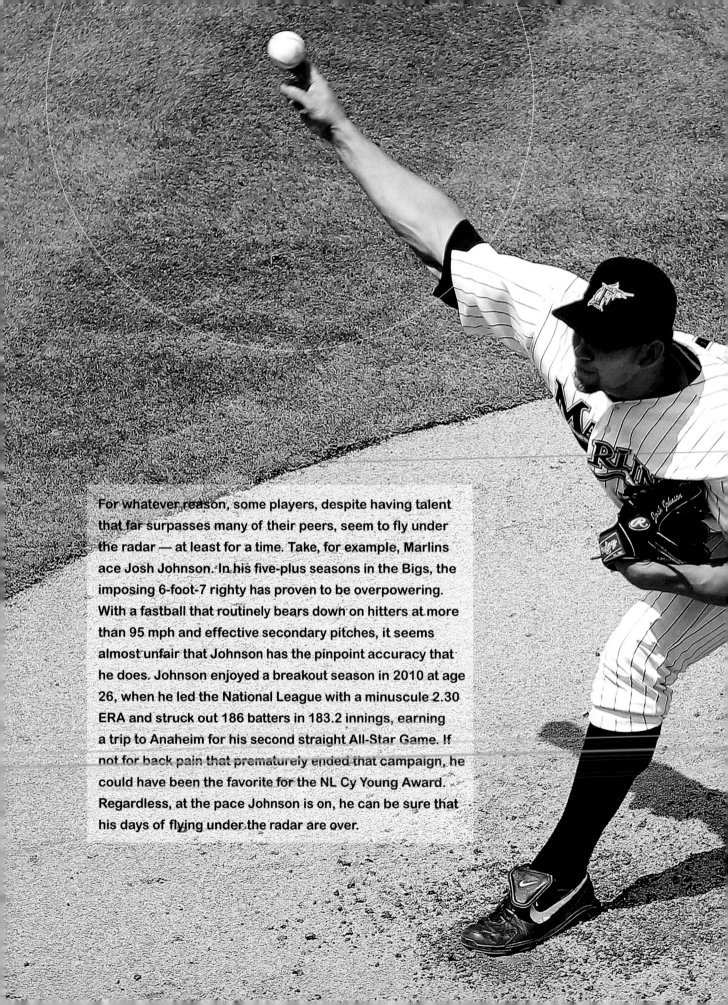

For whatever reason, some players, despite having talent that far surpasses many of their peers, seem to fly under the radar — at least for a time. Take, for example, Marlins ace Josh Johnson. In his five-plus seasons in the Bigs, the imposing 6-foot-7 righty has proven to be overpowering. With a fastball that routinely bears down on hitters at more than 95 mph and effective secondary pitches, it seems almost unfair that Johnson has the pinpoint accuracy that he does. Johnson enjoyed a breakout season in 2010 at age 26, when he led the National League with a minuscule 2.30 ERA and struck out 186 batters in 183.2 innings, earning a trip to Anaheim for his second straight All-Star Game. If not for back pain that prematurely ended that campaign, he could have been the favorite for the NL Cy Young Award. Regardless, at the pace Johnson is on, he can be sure that his days of flying under the radar are over.

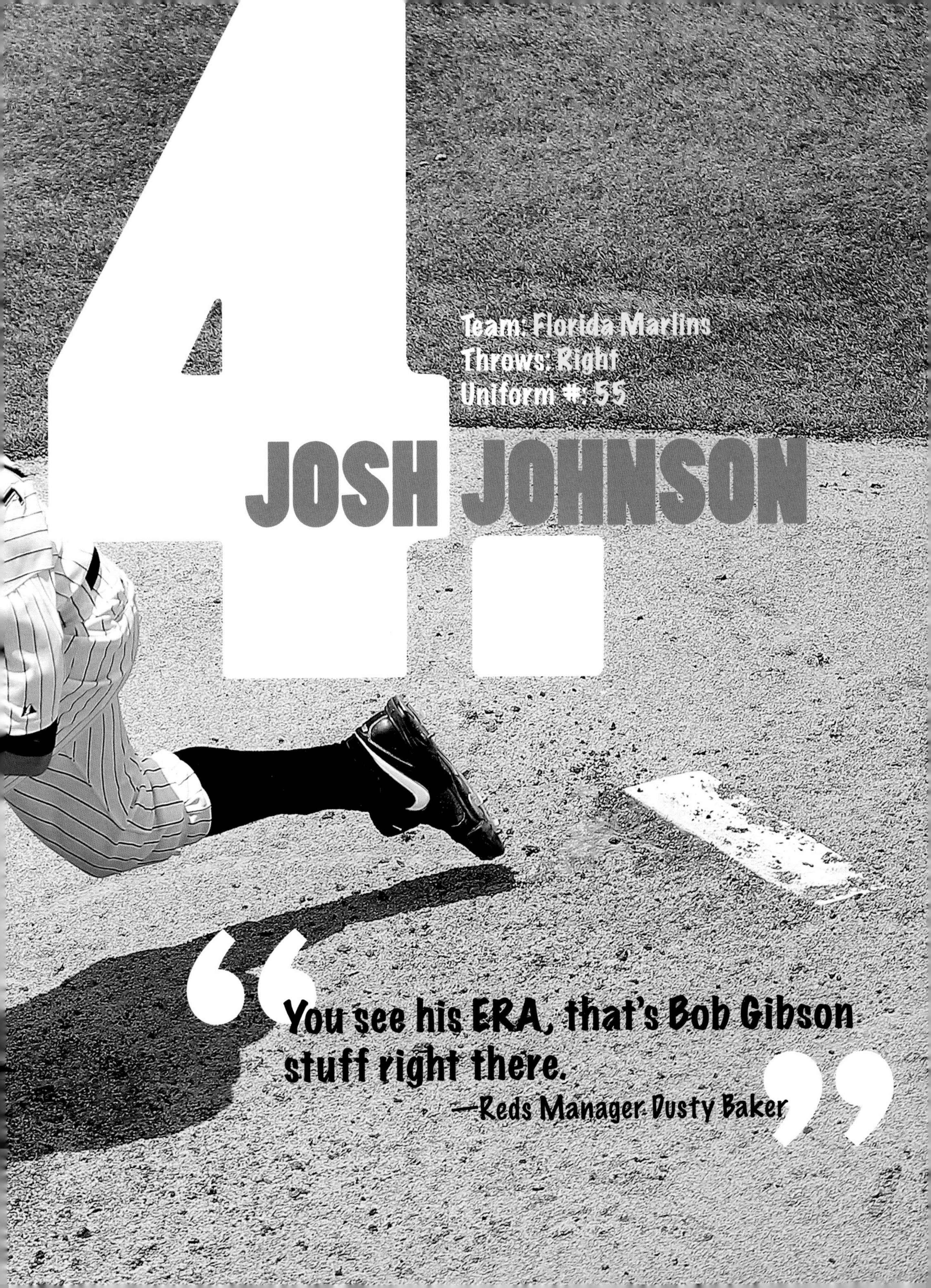

4

JOSH JOHNSON

Team: Florida Marlins
Throws: Right
Uniform #: 55

" You see his **ERA**, that's Bob Gibson stuff right there.
—Reds Manager Dusty Baker "

You might say that Phillies starter Cliff Lee was something of a late bloomer. After having moderate success early in his career, Lee hit a wall in 2007, posting an ERA greater than 6.00 and being demoted to the Minor Leagues. But during that stint in the Minors, Lee reinvented himself, adding a cut fastball to his arsenal of precisely located pitches. Lee returned to the Bigs in 2008, going 22-3 with a 2.54 ERA and winning the AL Cy Young Award with the Indians. The following season, the club dealt the left-hander to Philadelphia, where he went 4-0 in the playoffs and fell just short of leading the Phillies to their second straight World Series title. In 2010, after a quick stop in Seattle, Lee was on the move again, this time to Texas. As in Philadelphia, the southpaw came up big when it meant the most, winning all three of his ALDS and ALCS starts in lights-out fashion to guide the Rangers to their first-ever World Series berth. After the season, Lee signed a long-term deal to rejoin the Phillies and form — along with Roy Halladay, Roy Oswalt and Cole Hamels — one of the most formidable starting rotations in MLB history.

5. CLIFF LEE

Team: Philadelphia Phillies
Throws: Left
Uniform #: 33

6. JON LESTER

Team: Boston Red Sox
Throws: Left
Uniform #: 31

Dominance usually doesn't come without some adversity. For most top pitchers, this often means a stint in the Minors to work on mechanics or surgery to repair a damaged arm. But Red Sox starter Jon Lester's hardship was much more serious: He had to overcome cancer en route to stardom. In August 2006, the then–22-year-old left-hander was diagnosed with non-Hodgkin's lymphoma, thus cutting short his rookie season. After undergoing treatment, he returned the next season cancer-free and ready to take the Big Leagues by storm. Lester showed flashes of brilliance that year by going 4-0 in 11 starts. Then, in 2008, he threw the 18th no-hitter in Red Sox history and became a permanent fixture in the team's starting rotation. Two years later, he won 19 games, was an AL All-Star and established himself as the ace of a staff that included Josh Beckett, John Lackey and Daisuke Matsuzaka, three pitchers who have been dominant during their careers, as well. In 2010, at the age of 26, the 6-foot-4, 240-pound power pitcher led the league with 9.7 strikeouts per nine innings pitched.

FACTOID

Saved 12 games and didn't allow a run in the 1998 and '99 playoffs

7. MARIANO RIVERA

Team: New York Yankees
Throws: Right
Uniform #: 42

Perhaps no entrance music has ever been more appropriate for a player than Metallica's "Enter Sandman" is for closer Mariano Rivera; when he takes the mound, opposing fans might as well turn the game off and go to sleep, knowing that a Yankees win is a lock. Fans and hitters alike agree that the Panama native's nearly unhittable cutter is the best in the game. "He is the best modern-day weapon I have ever seen or played against," Alex Rodriguez says. "He has been the heart and soul of the New York Yankees dynasty." Indeed, Rivera has been part of every Yankees championship since 1996, winning the World Series MVP Award in 1999 after not allowing a run in eight postseason appearances that year. The perennial All-Star has led the Major Leagues in saves three times in his career, which has spanned the better part of two decades, and is widely regarded as the best in baseball history at his craft. And Mo has only gotten better with age, posting a sub-2.00 ERA almost every season since his 35th birthday in 2004.

8. JUSTIN VERLANDER

Team: Detroit Tigers
Throws: Right
Uniform #: 35

It doesn't always take time or adversity to develop into a dominant Big League pitcher. Some players, like the Tigers' Justin Verlander, attain the status right from the start. In 2006, the 6-foot-5 strikeout specialist won AL Rookie of the Year honors and helped lead Detroit to the World Series for the first time in 20-plus seasons, starting Game 1 against the Cardinals. In his sophomore year in the Bigs, Verlander threw the first no-hitter at Comerica Park (he would repeat the feat in 2011). And after hitting a speed bump in 2008, the towering right-hander surged in 2009, leading the AL in wins (19), innings pitched (240) and strikeouts (269). Of course, it doesn't hurt if you can hit 100 mph on the radar gun and maintain that velocity throughout the game. "I've never had a starting pitcher who could throw 99 [mph] in the ninth inning," Tigers Manager Jim Leyland says. Until he had Justin Verlander on his staff.

STAT CHART	Verlander's No-hitters	IP	H	R	ER	BB	K
	June 12, 2007	9	0	0	0	4	12
	May 7, 2011	9	0	0	0	1	4

9. CC SABATHIA

Team: New York Yankees
Throws: Left
Uniform #: 52

It's one thing to attain dominance — it's quite another to *maintain* it. CC Sabathia (the CC stands for Carsten Charles) knows a bit about both. The 6-foot-7 southpaw arrived at the Yankees' Spring Training facilities in Tampa, Fla., in 2011 after shedding 25 pounds thanks to an overhaul of his diet, in which candy and Cap'n Crunch cereal had become staples. With a renewed commitment to his physical fitness regimen, Sabathia instituted his lifestyle changes following what was arguably the most dominant season of his career until that point, when he led the American League with 21 wins and finished in the top four in Cy Young voting for the second straight year, after winning it in 2007 with the Indians. The seasons are rare in which Sabathia does not rank among league leaders in multiple pitching categories. And his assault on opposing batters comes with the pressure of playing for a pennant, as well; the 2009 ALCS MVP carried his team to the playoffs in five of his first ten Big League seasons.

10. JERED WEAVER

Team: Los Angeles Angels
Throws: Right
Uniform #: 36

The biggest expectation that falls on a team's ace is that when he takes the mound every fifth day his club *will* go home a winner. By that logic, the Los Angeles Angels have an ace in Jered Weaver who consistently lives up to high expectations. The California native — younger brother of former Major Leaguer Jeff Weaver — posted a .642 career winning percentage in his first 150 Big League starts. Drafted by the Angels out of Long Beach State with the 12th overall pick in the 2004 Draft, he ascended to the Majors less than a year later and has been a reliable moundsman ever since. And in 2010, Weaver, who went on to lead the Junior Circuit with a career-high 233 strikeouts on the season, reached a personal milestone as he made his first career All-Star Game appearance in front of a hometown crowd in Anaheim.

11. CLAYTON KERSHAW

Team: Los Angeles Dodgers
Throws: Left
Uniform #: 22

Early in his career, big things were expected from Clayton Kershaw, who was the Dodgers' first-round draft pick in 2006. A tall southpaw with a blazing fastball and nasty curveball, he inevitably drew comparisons to Dodgers legend Sandy Koufax when he made his Major League debut at age 20 in 2008. Yet despite the sky-high expectations, Kershaw has kept his cool and has not strayed from the plan, emerging as the ace of a talented Los Angeles pitching staff. Kershaw topped 200 innings pitched for the first time in 2010 while compiling a 2.91 ERA and striking out more than a batter per inning for the second straight season. With one of the best young arms in the Major Leagues, Kershaw should be a stalwart in the Dodgers' rotation for many years to come.

"I think we know what we've got," Dodgers Manager Don Mattingly says with assurance. "It's not so much the success, but it's the times in the past when I've seen him struggle with a rough outing and it doesn't affect him the next time. That's when you know you've got a kid that's confident in what he can do. That's what we expect, really. Every time he goes out there you expect to win."

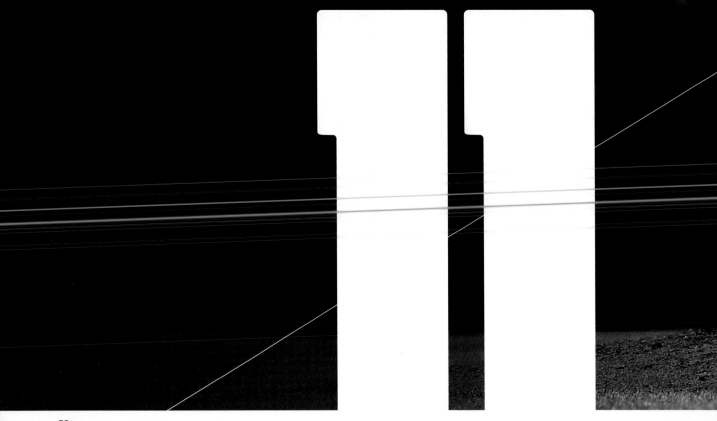

> ## "He's got a chance to rewrite a lot of the record books if he stays healthy. I would *expect* him to do so."
>
> —Rays pitching coach Jim Hickey

12. DAVID PRICE

Team: Tampa Bay Rays
Throws: Left
Uniform #: 14

Like the Cardinals' Adam Wainwright a few years before him, the Rays' David Price was a highly touted starter used as the team's closer before being moved into the rotation. The No. 1 overall pick of the 2007 Draft out of Vanderbilt University, Price quickly rose through the Rays' farm system and was saving games during Tampa's run to its first World Series in 2008. The next season, Price, a 6-foot-6, 225-pound left-hander who throws in the mid-90s, became a regular starter and his career continued as it was originally envisioned. He made 23 starts and struck out at least five batters in a game 10 times, winning 10 games for a Rays team that just missed the playoffs. In his sophomore campaign in 2010, the then–24-year-old was commanding, winning 19 games and posting a 2.72 ERA. Deservedly, he was the AL starter in the 2010 All-Star Game and finished second in AL Cy Young Award voting.

At one point in his life, it appeared as though Ubaldo Jimenez was destined to become a doctor in his native Dominican Republic. It's clear now, though, that he made an appropriate career choice, as he induces — rather than alleviates — pain among opposing batters. With one of baseball's most impressive fastballs, Jimenez has been a handful for hitters since his first full Major League season in 2008. "Ubaldo's just filthy — there's no way around that," longtime Rockies first baseman Todd Helton says. "He throws 97–98 mph and has good off-speed pitches. He stops losing streaks, and that's big." Jimenez broke out in the first half of 2010. In that half-season, the 6-foot-4 righty went 15-1 with a 2.20 ERA. These stats are especially impressive considering he pitches in one of baseball's best hitters parks — Coors Field. With that outstanding performance, Jimenez emerged as a household name for sports fans across the country and earned the start at the 2010 All-Star Game over several more established stars, such as Roy Halladay, Tim Lincecum and Adam Wainwright. With the stuff he's got, Jimenez can rack up the W's in any ballpark.

13. UBALDO JIMENEZ

Team: Colorado Rockies
Throws: Right
Uniform #: 38

FACTOID
Threw the first no-hitter in Rockies franchise history

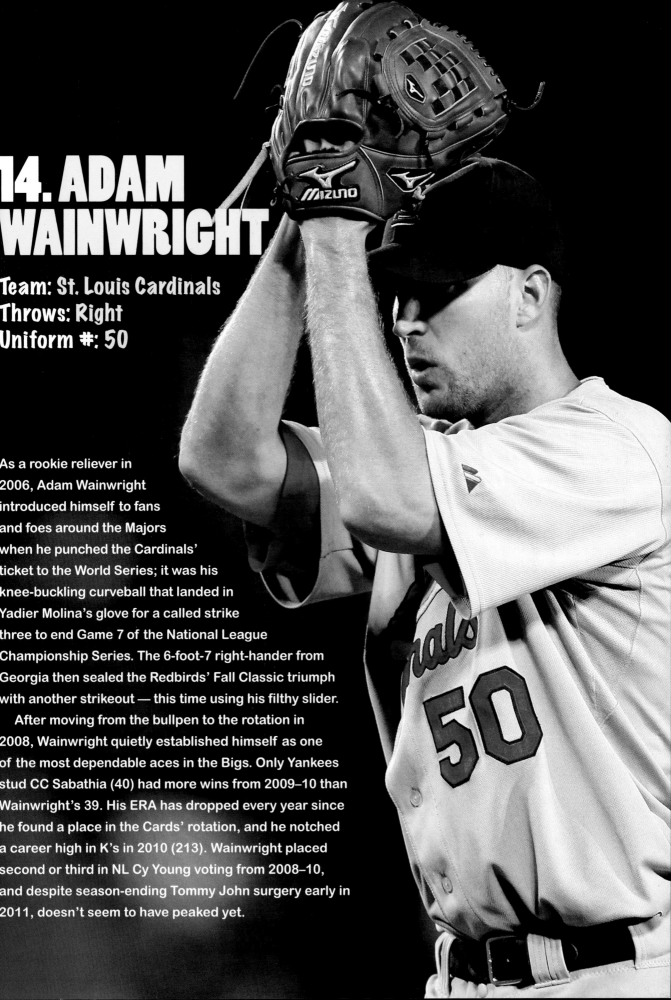

14. ADAM WAINWRIGHT

Team: St. Louis Cardinals
Throws: Right
Uniform #: 50

As a rookie reliever in 2006, Adam Wainwright introduced himself to fans and foes around the Majors when he punched the Cardinals' ticket to the World Series; it was his knee-buckling curveball that landed in Yadier Molina's glove for a called strike three to end Game 7 of the National League Championship Series. The 6-foot-7 right-hander from Georgia then sealed the Redbirds' Fall Classic triumph with another strikeout — this time using his filthy slider.

After moving from the bullpen to the rotation in 2008, Wainwright quietly established himself as one of the most dependable aces in the Bigs. Only Yankees stud CC Sabathia (40) had more wins from 2009–10 than Wainwright's 39. His ERA has dropped every year since he found a place in the Cards' rotation, and he notched a career high in K's in 2010 (213). Wainwright placed second or third in NL Cy Young voting from 2008–10, and despite season-ending Tommy John surgery early in 2011, doesn't seem to have peaked yet.

15. BRIAN WILSON

Team: San Francisco Giants
Throws: Right
Uniform #: 38

15

Wilson's outlandish off-field antics — such as appearing on a late-night TV talk show dressed like a 19th-century sea captain — sometimes distract from just how great he can be on the mound. But there is no question that the Giants' eccentric closer exploded into a full-blown media sensation in the aftermath of San Francisco's 2010 world championship. Not only does Wilson march to the beat of his own drum, but during the team's title run he managed to become the Pied Piper of San Francisco, as shoe-polish hued beards popped up in the AT&T Park bullpen and throughout the Bay Area.

On the way to the Giants' first victory parade since moving to San Francisco, opponents took note to "Fear the Beard" — they just couldn't do anything about it. Wilson mowed down hitters in 2010, recording one of the best seasons ever by a closer by saving a Major League–leading 48 games. Without an offensive juggernaut supporting him, Wilson's ability to slam the door shut has been of the utmost importance. With a blazing fastball and nasty off-speed pitches, he has struck out more than a batter per inning during his career.

FACTOID
Inspired the "Fear the Beard" slogan among San Francisco Giants fans

Despite playing for a young team in a small market, Joakim Soria has established himself as one of baseball's most dominant closers, up there with household names like Mariano and Papelbon. Armed with a slow curveball that keeps hitters off balance, Soria has turned ninth-inning Royals leads into something of a guarantee, blowing a mere nine saves over the course of his first three years as the team's full-time closer. In that span, the Mexico-born right-hander successfully put the lid on a remarkable 115 games, racking up more than nine strikeouts per nine innings on average. In 2010, Soria posted a microscopic 1.78 ERA (fourth best in the American League among relievers) while saving 43 games (also second best) in 46 opportunities, and he has already earned multiple All-Star Game selections. Although the rebuilding Royals have struggled to pick up wins in recent years, Soria has given everyone throughout Kansas City — his teammates, coaches and the fans — confidence that if the Royals take a lead into the ninth, it's lights out for their opponent.

STAT CHART

	ERA	SV	IP	K	K/9
2008	1.60	42	67.1	66	8.8
2009	2.21	30	53.0	69	11.7
2010	1.78	43	65.2	71	9.7

16. JOAKIM SORIA

Team: Kansas City Royals
Throws: Right
Uniform #: 48

17. DAN HAREN

Team: Los Angeles Angels
Throws: Right
Uniform #: 24

If your plan for an at-bat against Dan Haren is to work the count, there's a good chance you'll go down 0-2 before you've even had time to adjust your batting gloves. A master of command, Haren ranks among the top 10 in Big League history in strikeout-to-walk ratio and has also racked up 200 strikeouts several times, thanks in large part to some of the filthiest movement in the Majors on his breaking pitches. "I think one of the reasons Haren has separated himself is he's always pounding the strike zone,"

says Rangers star Michael Young. "It seems like every time you go up there, it's strike one."

The All-Star regular consistently logs 200-plus innings while making at least 30 starts every season and has led staffs in Oakland and Arizona. In 2010 he was traded to the Angels — amazingly the third time he was dealt since the Cardinals drafted him in 2001. He picked up right where he left off, recording a 2.87 ERA in 14 starts during what was considered, for him, to be a down year.

18. ZACK GREINKE

Team: Milwaukee Brewers
Throws: Right
Uniform #: 13

As the sixth overall pick in the 2002 Draft, Zack Greinke was expected to be an elite starting pitcher almost immediately. But the 6-foot-2 right-hander had personal hurdles to overcome before reaching that superstar potential. Once back on the mound, though, Greinke managed to draw national attention despite pitching away from the spotlight in Kansas City. With a hard fastball, perhaps the best slider in the game and excellent control, Greinke displays all the tools a pitcher could ask for. He finished 2008 with 14 scoreless frames and began 2009 with 24 more for a remarkable total of 38 straight. He finished the '09 season with a league-leading 2.16 ERA and 16 victories for a last-place team. That performance was strong enough to earn Greinke an AL Cy Young Award and establish his rank as one of baseball's top starters. Prior to the 2011 season, Greinke was traded to the Milwaukee Brewers. Now with a powerful offense behind him, he can be expected to continue to battle for many more honors in the future.

19. MATT CAIN

Team: San Francisco Giants
Throws: Right
Uniform #: 18

When the Giants won the 2010 World Series, most of the accolades went to the charismatic two-time Cy Young–winning Tim Lincecum for his phenomenal post-season performance and electric pitching style, and to eccentric closer Brian Wilson for his wild looks and shutdown ninth innings. But Giants No. 2 starter Matt Cain deserves just as much credit for bringing a world championship to the City by the Bay.

In three postseason starts, Cain did not allow an earned run and gave up just 13 hits in 21.1 innings, earning the nickname "Big Game Cain" from Giants fans. But the postseason success was not a mirage. The 6-foot-3, 230-pound righty has used an overpowering fastball and outstanding slider to dominate hitters ever since he came up to the Big Leagues in 2005 — and he has an All-Star resume to show for it. Whether he garners the attention that he deserves or not, Cain — still a few years from his 30th birthday — is undeniably an integral part of the Giants' recent success and should continue to mow down Senior Circuit hitters for years to come.

STAT CHART	W	L	IP	ERA	K
2010	0	0	6.2	0.00	6
NLDS	0	0	7.0	0.00	5
NLCS	1	0	7.2	0.00	2
WS	1	0			

20. NEFTALI FELIZ

Team: Texas Rangers
Throws: Right
Uniform #: 30

When the Rangers called Neftali Feliz up from the Minor Leagues in August 2009, they could not have expected such dominance from the then–20-year-old pitcher. All Feliz did was throw 31 innings over the final two months of the season, allowing a measly 13 hits while striking out an impressive 39 batters. Because of that performance, Feliz was named the Rangers' full-time closer in 2010, and he has never looked back. In his first season in the role, the Dominican right-hander successfully finished off 40 of 43 save opportunities and held opposing hitters to a .176 average en route to the AL Rookie of the Year Award. There is no debate as to what makes Feliz so successful. Standing 6 foot 3, he overpowers hitters with a fastball that typically blazes by them at more than 95 mph. Feliz also throws a quality breaking ball to offset the heat. And he's clutch, too: In the 2010 postseason, the rookie posted a 1.23 ERA over 7.1 innings to help bring the Rangers all the way to their first-ever World Series appearance.

FACTOID
First Rangers pitcher ever to win the Rookie of the Year Award

21. STEPHEN STRASBURG

Team: Washington Nationals
Throws: Right
Uniform #: 37

As a high school phenom in the San Diego area, Stephen Strasburg caught the eye of Hall of Famer Tony Gwynn, who would coach the right-hander at San Diego State University. Strasburg then caught the public eye in his junior year, striking out 195 batters in 109 innings with a triple-digit fastball and a wicked slider. He would become the No. 1 overall pick of the 2009 Draft, debuting a little more than a year after being selected in front of a capacity crowd at Washington's Nationals Park, where he gave up just two runs in seven innings. Much of America tuned in to witness this most dominant of debuts. The game, shown live nationally on MLB Network, was the highest-rated telecast in the network's history. It was also the highest-rated Nationals game ever on MASN2, the local sports network in the Washington, D.C., area. In 12 starts in 2010, Strasburg went 5-3 with a 2.91 ERA and 92 K's in 68 frames before undergoing Tommy John surgery to repair a torn ligament in his right elbow. But the 6-foot-4 right-hander still has a long career ahead of him, much to the chagrin of opposing hitters across the Majors.

Magic Number

14

Strasburg's strikeout total in his MLB debut

Every career is unique in its own way. There are some pitchers who seem destined to be stars from the second they make their Major League debuts. Then there are those like Chris Carpenter whose careers take a little more time to develop. Although the 6-foot-6, 230-pound right-hander didn't break out until the age of 29, when he went 15-5 with a 3.46 ERA in his first season with the Cards, he quickly established himself as a perennial Cy Young contender. Under the tutelage of pitching coach Dave Duncan, Carpenter — an intense competitor — won the award in 2005 by going 21-5 with a 2.83 ERA and leading the league with seven complete games. In 2006, when the Cardinals won the World Series, Carpenter threw eight scoreless innings to pick up one of the team's four wins. Even though Carpenter developed late in his career, he kept working hard to achieve the highest accolades that a pitcher can. "He's fearless out there," says former Cardinals teammate Jason Isringhausen. "He just goes after hitters and doesn't back down for anything."

22. CHRIS CARPENTER

Team: St. Louis Cardinals
Throws: Right
Uniform #: 29

23. HEATH BELL

Team: San Diego Padres
Throws: Right
Uniform #: 21

Since taking over closing duties from Padres legend and all-time Major League saves king Trevor Hoffman at the start of the 2009 campaign, Bell has been one of the most reliable end-game options in the Major Leagues. He locked down a National League–leading 42 games in his first year with the coveted gig and then an eye-popping 47 games the next season. Although the power pitcher may have taken a circuitous route to the ninth inning in San Diego, his fastball wastes no time finding the catcher's mitt. Punching out more than a batter per inning over the course of his career, Bell re- lies heavily on a heater that sits between 93 and 94 mph while mixing in a nasty curveball. Standing 6 foot 3 and weighing upwards of 250 pounds, this right-hander is quite a presence on the mound.

FACTOID
Converted 89 of 98 save chances in his first two years as the Padres' closer

Whichever scout in the Cincinnati Reds organization first informed General Manager Walt Jocketty about the talents of this Cuban flamethrower must have felt something like Santa Claus delivering the perfect gift on Christmas eve. In 2010, Chapman registered what was then the fastest recorded pitch of all time — a fastball to Tony Gwynn Jr. that was clocked at a mindblowing 105.1 mph — in just his 11th Major League appearance. "You're not even going to put the bat on the ball [at that speed]," Gwynn told reporters. The next season, Chapman's record was broken — by, who else, himself, when he had one pitch clocked at 106 mph against the Pittsburgh Pirates.

While the "Cuban Missile's" heater may not be traveling as fast as a speeding bullet, it's not too far behind. And both are far in the rear view of his already growing reputation. Used in middle relief in his debut season, Chapman's future is bright. The long and lean left-hander dazzled in an abbreviated 15 appearances, striking out 19, short-circuiting a few radar guns and showing a clear sign of what's to come.

24. AROLDIS CHAPMAN

Team: Cincinnati Reds
Throws: Left
Uniform #: 54

25. JONATHAN BROXTON

Team: Los Angeles Dodgers
Throws: Right
Uniform #: 51

Commanding the ninth inning of a Big League game is nearly as much about presence as it is about talent. Whether it's the placid demeanor of Mariano Rivera or the whirling dervish motion of Francisco Rodriguez, big-time closers have a way of getting attention. Towering at 6 foot 4 and tipping the scales at close to 300 pounds, Broxton looks more like an NFL lineman or a professional wrestler than a hurler when he takes the mound.

But with a fastball that can get up there in the high 90s, it's obvious he's a star at his craft. The fireballing Broxton averaged better than 11 K's per nine frames in his first five seasons as a major contributor with the Dodgers. Broxton laid claim to the Dodgers' closing gig in 2009 when he locked down 36 saves while striking out an unfathomable 114 batters in just 76 innings of work. With numbers like that, hitters can consider themselves fortunate to so much as put the ball in play.

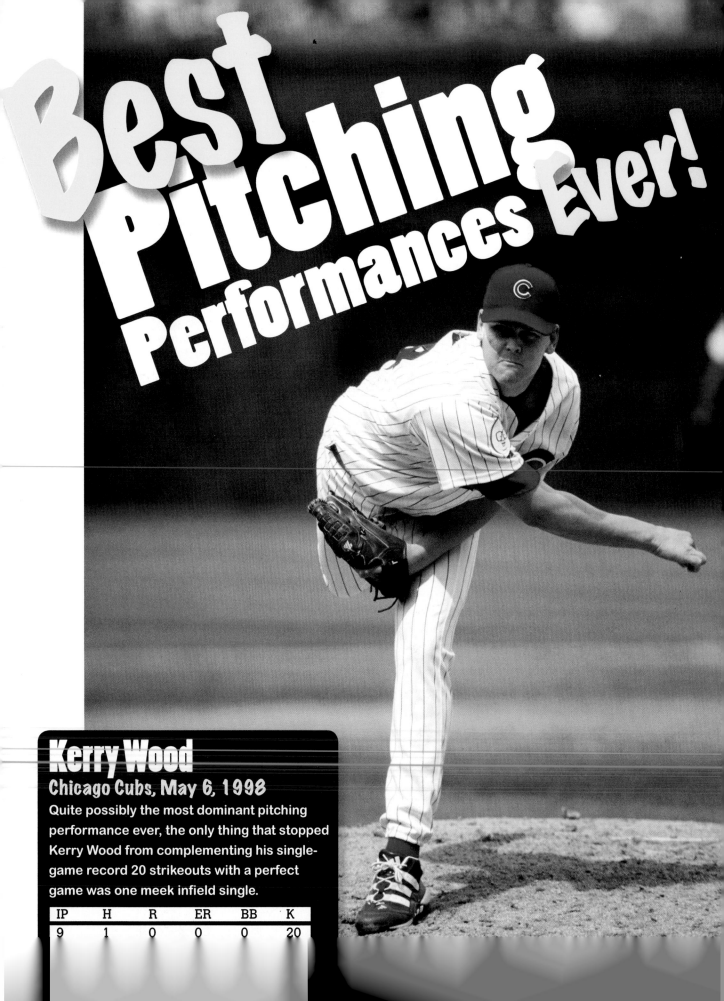

Best Pitching Performances Ever!

Kerry Wood
Chicago Cubs, May 6, 1998

Quite possibly the most dominant pitching performance ever, the only thing that stopped Kerry Wood from complementing his single-game record 20 strikeouts with a perfect game was one meek infield single.

IP	H	R	ER	BB	K
9	1	0	0	0	20

Don Larsen
New York Yankees, Oct. 8, 1956
World Series Game 5

Don Larsen didn't learn that he would be starting Game 5 against the Dodgers until he arrived at the ballpark. But he pitched like he had prepared for the moment his entire life, throwing the first and only perfect game in Fall Classic history.

IP	H	R	ER	BB	K
9	0	0	0	0	7

Bob Gibson
St. Louis Cardinals, Oct. 2, 1968
World Series Game 1

In the original "Year of the Pitcher," 1968 NL Cy Young winner — and arguably the most intimidating hurler of all time — Bob Gibson continued his supremacy over the opposition, setting a record for strikeouts in a World Series game with 17.

IP	H	R	ER	BB	K
9	5	0	0	1	17

Roy Halladay
Philadelphia Phillies, Oct. 6, 2010
NLDS Game 1

Making the first postseason start of his illustrious career at the age of 33, Roy Halladay appeared unfazed by the spotlight, shutting down the powerful Cincinnati Reds — the NL's highest scoring offense — with just the second no-hitter in postseason history.

IP	H	R	ER	BB	K
9	0	0	0	1	8

Harvey Haddix
Pittsburgh Pirates, May 26, 1959

If Harvey Haddix's unmatched outing against the Milwaukee Braves isn't the greatest pitching performance ever, it's certainly the greatest outing in a loss. The lefty threw a remarkable 12 perfect frames before an error in the 13th inning led to the first Braves base runner and, ultimately, the winning run for Milwaukee.

IP	H	R	ER	BB	K
12.2	1	1	0	1	8

Jack Morris

Minnesota Twins, Oct. 27, 1991
World Series Game 7

There's always debate as to whether Jack Morris should be a Hall of Famer, with much of his case resting on his stellar postseason performances, highlighted by this gem in the most pressure-packed situation of all. Morris worked overtime for the Twins to seal the championship with a 1-0 victory.

IP	H	R	ER	BB	K
10	7	0	0	2	8

Johnny Vander Meer

Cincinnati Reds
June 11 and June 15, 1938

Technically it was over two outings, but what Reds lefty Johnny Vander Meer accomplished in consecutive starts in 1938 is unthinkable. On June 11, he no-hit the Boston Braves in a 3-0 win. One start later, he did the same against the Brooklyn Dodgers in a 6-0 victory.

IP	H	R	ER	BB	K
9	0	0	0	3	4
9	0	0	0	8	7

MOUND

Now that you've read about the Most Feared Pitchers in Major League Baseball, you can use these stat sheets to track your favorite hurlers throughout the Big League season. Using a pencil, fill in the stats below for your favorite pitchers.

PITCHER TRACKER

PLAYER	W–L	IP	ERA	K	BB	SV
Roy Halladay						
Felix Hernandez						
Tim Lincecum						
Josh Johnson						
Cliff Lee						
Jon Lester						
Mariano Rivera						
Justin Verlander						
CC Sabathia						
Jered Weaver						
Clayton Kershaw						
David Price						
Ubaldo Jimenez						
Adam Wainwright						
Brian Wilson						
Joakim Soria						
Dan Haren						

TRACKER

Enter even more players' names into the empty spaces and use the grid to keep an eye on their numbers, as well. This way you can follow other hurlers vying to be one of Major League Baseball's Most Feared Pitchers.

PITCHER TRACKER						
PLAYER	W–L	IP	ERA	K	BB	SV
Zack Greinke						
Matt Cain						
Neftali Feliz						
Stephen Strasburg						
Chris Carpenter						
Heath Bell						
Aroldis Chapman						
Jonathan Broxton						

Fun and Games

Hidden in the grid below are the last names of 10 of Major League Baseball's Most Feared Pitchers. Their names may be found listed in any direction: forward, backward, up, down and diagonally. How many can you find?

W	I	L	S	O	N	G	T	V	A	J	R
E	A	R	B	X	E	W	M	K	O	Q	E
A	E	I	I	E	R	Y	H	I	A	Z	T
V	K	Y	N	W	A	E	X	S	G	B	S
E	F	L	T	W	H	E	C	A	O	N	E
R	O	I	G	E	R	K	D	B	E	L	L
D	E	N	H	I	E	I	M	A	I	U	L
G	M	C	V	U	J	E	G	T	H	C	Z
E	U	E	N	A	M	P	A	H	C	Q	Q
A	R	C	T	B	C	S	U	I	T	M	L
A	K	U	B	S	A	R	O	A	Q	F	D
C	E	M	T	A	N	P	E	R	V	B	T

(Heath) BELL

(Aroldis) CHAPMAN

(Dan) HAREN

(Jon) LESTER

(Tim) LINCECUM

(Mariano) RIVERA

(CC) SABATHIA

(Adam) WAINWRIGHT

(Jered) WEAVER

(Brian) WILSON

MATCHING Match the current or former pitching great with his nickname.

1.	Nolan Ryan	A.	Sandman
2.	Roy Halladay	B.	The Big Unit
3.	Dontrelle Willis	C.	The Express
4.	Greg Maddux	D.	D-Train
5.	Randy Johnson	E.	Sweet Music
6.	Frank Viola	F.	Doc
7.	Tim Lincecum	G.	The Freak
8.	Mariano Rivera	H.	King
9.	Roger Clemens	I.	Mad Dog
10.	Felix Hernandez	J.	The Rocket

PITCHING LINGO In the space provided, define each pitching term.

1. Hook _____

2. Ace _____

3. Hill _____

4. Heater _____

5. Chin music _____

6. Punchout _____

7. Beanball _____

8. Battery _____

9. Set-up man _____

10. Southpaw _____

All answers on page 48.

Fun and Games
answers

WORD SEARCH

W	I	L	S	O	N	G	T	V	A	J	R
E	A	R	B	X	E	W	M	K	O	Q	E
A	E	I	I	E	R	Y	H	I	A	Z	T
V	K	Y	N	W	A	E	X	S	G	B	S
E	F	L	T	W	H	E	C	A	O	N	E
R	O	I	G	E	R	K	D	B	E	L	L
D	E	N	H	I	E	I	M	A	I	U	L
G	M	C	V	U	J	E	G	T	H	C	Z
E	U	E	N	A	M	P	A	H	C	Q	Q
A	R	C	T	B	C	S	U	I	T	M	L
A	K	U	B	S	A	R	O	A	Q	F	D
C	E	M	T	A	N	P	E	R	V	B	T

MATCHING
1. C; 2. F; 3. D; 4. I; 5. B; 6. E; 7. G; 8. A; 9. J; 10. H

PITCHING LINGO
1. curveball; 2. team's best starting pitcher; 3. pitcher's mound; 4. fastball; 5. high and inside pitch; 6. strikeout; 7. pitch that hits a batter; 8. pitcher-catcher combination; 9. relief pitcher who enters the game before the closer; 10. left-handed pitcher

THE MAJOR LEAGUE BASEBALL

25

MOST FEARED PITCHERS